FRANK LLOYD WRIGHT

on Architecture, Nature, and the Human Spirit
A Collection of Quotations

Edited by Bruce Brooks Pfeiffer

First Galison edition, published in 2016.

Design by Galison | www.galison.com
Galison 70 W 36th Street New York, NY 10018

This Frank Lloyd Wright Foundation product is authorized by the Frank Lloyd
Wright Foundation, Taliesin West, Scottsdale, Arizona, USA. "Frank Lloyd Wright" is
a trademark of the Frank Lloyd Wright Foundation and is used with permission. A
portion of the proceeds from this product supports the conservation and education
programs of the Foundation. www.franklloydwright.org

ISBN 978-0-7353-4826-4

The Library of Congress has cataloged the previous edition as follows:

Wright, Frank Lloyd, 1867–1959.
    Frank Lloyd Wright on architecture, nature, and the human spirit :
a collection of quotations / edited by Bruce Brooks Pfeiffer.
        p. cm.
Includes bibliographical references.
ISBN 978-0-7649-5956-1 (hardcover)
I. Wright, Frank Lloyd, 1867–1959—Quotations. I. Pfeiffer, Bruce Brooks. II. Title.

NA737.W7A35 2011
720.92—dc22

                            2011009647

Printed in China

2 3 4 5 6 7 8 9 10

TABLE OF CONTENTS

INTRO
DUCTION

FRANK LLOYD WRIGHT was unquestionably the most prominent, revered, and gifted architect of his time—if not, arguably, of all time. He is well known for buildings in the United States as well as in Japan, and his reputation has been reinforced by the hundreds of unbuilt designs that can be seen and studied in the many books about his work published worldwide. He not only produced great architecture, in all categories, from the smallest home to a civic center of sizable proportions; he also wrote and spoke copiously about the art and craft of architecture, the fine arts, urbanism, and society. Among his most important writings are an autobiography and the many lectures he delivered in the United States and in England. His thoughts on the nature of materials, published in *The Architectural Record* in 1927 and 1928, were an early contribution to this genre. The book *A Testament*, which appeared in 1957, was part autobiography, part philosophy, and part architectural treatise.

Wright called his architecture "organic," an approach he defined in several different ways during his lifetime—it proceeded from within outward; each part was to the other parts as the whole was to its constituents; it was of its time; it was of its place; and it was meant to provide an environment of beauty for the life of mankind.

His books and public lectures were devoted to these concepts, and for him architecture was always the frame for life. "Architecture must now construct anew the whole social pattern of our time as a new order of the human spirit."[1]

He also defined his chosen art form as "that great living creative spirit which from generation to generation, from age to age, proceeds, persists, creates, according to the nature of man and his circumstances as they both *change*."[2]

"The architect," wrote Wright on another occasion, "must be the master in the interior sense, not only of his tools, not only of his materials, but also of the human spirit. The soul of humanity is in his charge, really."[3]

And, nearly as grandly, "Man takes a positive hand in creation whenever he puts a building upon the earth beneath the sun. If he has any birthright at all, it must consist in this, that he, too, is no less a feature of the landscape than the rocks, trees, bears, or bees of that nature to which he owes his being."[4]

His interests and deep concerns went beyond architecture to embrace the realms of ethics, existence, and all aspects of human behavior. In this sense, he was truly the proverbial Renaissance man. His thoughts on all these topics can be found in the writings ostensibly devoted to architecture. There is, however, another category of his writings that is far more personal—the Sunday morning talks to the apprentices who made up the Taliesin Fellowship.

The talks were a tradition at Taliesin, Wright's home and studio in southwestern Wisconsin, as well as at Taliesin West, his winter compound in Arizona. Wright and his wife, Olgivanna, would join the members of the fellowship for Sunday morning breakfast, and at the conclusion of the meal the room would grow quiet as all waited for Wright to speak. "Quiet seems to be descending upon the house," said Wright on one of these occasions. "When quiet descends, I suppose it's an invitation for somebody to speak, and I'm afraid that somebody is me."[5] "You know, I am getting into the position of a preacher. My father was a preacher and I remember going with my mother to church every Sunday morning and sitting down below and seeing him up in the pulpit, and here I am getting dangerously near to the similar circumstances. I don't propose to be a preacher, just as you know I don't propose to be a teacher either—except by example."[6]

Another tradition at Taliesin was the Saturday evening dinner followed by a film, booked specially for the occasion and shown in the Taliesin Playhouse with its 35mm projectors. These films came from all the major Hollywood studios, and also from France, Czechoslovakia, Italy, and Russia. Frequently a Sunday morning talk began with a review of the film shown the night before. The day after *Prelude to Fame* was shown, Wright remarked, "It is refreshing to see a movie that has in it not only something of an idea, but human sympathies and justice working out. It was charming to see that everybody in that film last night got what was coming to him."[7]

Despite his reluctance to be either a preacher or a teacher, Wright's Sunday morning talks were definitely in the nature of sermons, and regardless of his protestations, the architect was certainly imparting wisdom and serious advice. Both he and Olgivanna felt a profound sense of responsibility toward the young men and women of the fellowship, an extended family in which the Wrights acted as parents.

To assemble the current book, I combed through Wright's published writings. The other important source is those Sunday morning talks. Soon after I joined the Taliesin Fellowship in the winter of 1949, I began to regret that his words shared with the fellows, which left a deep impression on me, were being lost. Even though the talks were impromptu, they struck me as too valuable to perish. Accordingly, I acquired a tape recorder and began recording. Over the next ten years, we upgraded tape recorders several times to assure the highest quality of recording possible. During that remarkable decade, we amassed approximately 250 hours of Frank Lloyd Wright on tape. Eventually we made tape-to-tape copies, which are available for study and research today. Transcripts of the tapes provided many of the quotations in the pages that follow— and in this introduction.

Wright once confessed: "I had to choose early in my life between an honest arrogance and a hypocritical humility and I deliberately chose an honest arrogance."[8] But he qualified that statement later, saying: "I have talked of honest arrogance, but there is no such thing as honest arrogance. Arrogance is only arrogance when it has nothing under it, when it has nothing to stand on, when it is a pretense, a quackery, or a fake. When it is genuine, it is a pride that is the highest form of humility we will ever know. It is evidence of a great faith in one's own ground, one's own star, a religious faith, perhaps, that cannot be broken down, and we should not call it arrogance."[9]

He expressed something similar when he said, "Your soul is the real you. The soul is the essence of you, the essential you. Your spirit is the temper, color, and expressiveness of your soul."[10]

On a more personal note, he also remarked:

"If you were to deduct Froebel, Goethe, Beethoven, and Nietzsche from my education I should be very much the poorer."[11]

"Of all the fine arts, music it was that I could not live without—as taught by my father (the symphony an edifice of sound). [I] found in it [a] sympathetic parallel to architecture. Beethoven and Bach were princely architects in my spiritual realm."[12]

In these excerpts from the Sunday morning talks a strong sense of ethics prevailed, and Wright clearly stated the difference between ethics and morals: "Morals are the customs which are conceded to be, or considered to be, the good ones as against the bad ones. When we say a moral man we mean a man who, according to the tenor and judgment of his time, does the right thing. But it may not be, in any ethical analysis, the true thing. When you speak of ethics, then you are getting to the actual organic nature of right and wrong. Ethics and morality have very little in common."[13] Giving a specific example, Wright pointed out that "the truly ethical person would be more in a fix than Jesus Himself was. He was truly ethical. You could not speak of Jesus as a moral man. That would be degrading. It would make Him of His time and of His day, which, of course, He was not."[14]

Although he deplored organized Christian religion, believing that it did not fully reflect the teachings of Jesus, Wright was basically a deeply religious person.

"The great thing for us is faith—faith in the incarnation—faith in its quality, in its inevitability, in its indestructibility. That is what we call religion—should call religion. And that religion is the greatest religion which gives you the most strength and courage in that faith."[15]

"There is nothing higher, that I can see, than the deep

and full understanding and appreciation of the beauty around you—the beauty of the idea we call Nature, the body, you might say, who made the body of God the Great Idea."[16]

Bruce Brooks Pfeiffer
Director Emeritus,
The Frank Lloyd Wright Archives
Frank Lloyd Wright Foundation

1. Frank Lloyd Wright, "Recollections—United States, 1893–1920," *Architects' Journal of London*, August 6, 1936, 174.

2. Frank Lloyd Wright, "An Organic Architecture," in *Collected Writings, Volume 3, 1931–1939,* ed. Bruce Brooks Pfeiffer (New York: Rizzoli, 1993), 331.

3. *Frank Lloyd Wright: His Living Voice*, selected and with commentary by Bruce Brooks Pfeiffer (Fresno: Press at California State University, Fresno, 1987), 206.

4. Baker Brownell and Frank Lloyd Wright, *Architecture and Modern Life* (New York: Harper, 1937), 19–20.

5. Transcript of tape recordings made of Frank Lloyd Wright speaking between 1949 and 1959, Frank Lloyd Wright Foundation Archives, Taliesin West, Scottsdale, Arizona, no. 145, 1 (hereafter this source is abbreviated as "TT").

6. TT no. 95, 1.

7. TT no. 29, 1.

8. TT no. 241, 12.

9. TT no. 286, 8.

10. TT no. 47, 20.

11. TT no. 129, 12.

12. Wright, *Testament*, 206.

13. TT no. 46, 8.

14. Ibid., 8–9.

15. TT no. 47, 23.

16. TT no. 214, 1.

ARCHITECTURE

DEFINITIONS

1930

Architecture is the triumph of human imagination over materials, methods, and men to put man into possession of his own earth.

1954

What does the word *architect* mean? The exact translation would be *the master of the know-how. Arch*—high, like archbishop, arch-this, arch-that. *Tect*—meaning technique, know-how. So you get *architect*—master of the know-how.

1959

There is no architecture without a philosophy. There is no art of any kind without its own philosophy.

1931

All the color and texture the eye has seen—all the rhythms the ear has heard—all the grace of form the mind may grasp—are properties of architecture.

ARCHITECTURE IS THE SCIENTIFIC ART OF MAKING STRUCTURE EXPRESS IDEAS.

1957

The mission of an architect is to help people understand how to make life more beautiful, the world a better one for living in, and to give reason, rhyme, and meaning to life.

1932

We have great bridges all over the world. A great bridge may be great architecture in the true sense, but the more they are let alone by architects the more they are great bridges.

1954

What is needed more in architecture—just what it is in human life—integrity.

1931

Whenever architecture was great it was modern, and whenever architecture was modern human values were the only values preserved.

What is architecture? I know that architecture is life; or at least it is life itself taking form and therefore is the truest record of life as it was lived in the world yesterday, as it is being lived today, or ever will be lived. Architecture is that great living creative spirit which from generation to generation, from age to age, proceeds, persists, creates, according to the nature of man, and his circumstances as they both change. That really is architecture.

1955

Architecture is the frame of life. It is the nature and substance of whatever is.

BUILDING IN NATURE

1931

A house, we like to believe, is in status quo a noble consort to man and the trees; therefore the house should have repose and such texture as will quiet the whole and make it graciously at one with external nature.

1954

I began to see a building primarily not as a cave but as broad shelter in the open, related to vista; vista without and vista within.

1937

Man takes a positive hand in creation whenever he puts a building upon the earth beneath the sun. If he has birthright at all, it must consist in this: that he, too, is no less a feature of the landscape than the rocks, trees, bears or bees of that nature to which he owes his being.

1957

The good building is not one that hurts the landscape, but is one that makes the landscape more beautiful than it was before that building was built.

1955

OF THE GROUND AND INTO THE LIGHT IS THE FIRST BASIS OF A GOOD HOUSE. LOOKING AT IT, YOU COULD NOT IMAGINE IT ANYWHERE BUT RIGHT THERE.

ORGANIC ARCHITECTURE

1914

By organic architecture I mean an architecture that *develops* from within outward in harmony with the conditions of its being, as distinguished from one that is *applied* from without.

1954

This gospel of organic architecture still has more in sympathy and in common with Oriental thought than it has with any other thing the West has confessed . . . It cannot truthfully be said, however, that organic architecture was derived from the Orient. We have our own way of putting these elemental (so ancient) ideals into practical effect . . . The idea of organic architecture that the reality of the building lies in the space within to be lived in, the feeling that we must not enclose ourselves in an envelope which is the building, is not alone Oriental. Democracy, proclaiming the integrity of the individual *per se,* had the feeling if not the words.

The proposed new building for the Guggenheim Museum
. . . is the latest sense of organic architecture. Here we are not
building a cellular composition of compartments, but one
where all is one great space on a single continuous floor. The
eye encounters no abrupt change, but is gently led and treated
as if at the edge of the shore watching an unbreaking wave.

Organic architecture is architecture in the reflex: architecture
that seeks to serve man rather than to become or be becoming
to one of those forces that try to rule over him.

Organic architecture is American architecture; it is America's
contribution to the architecture of the world. Not the Inter-
national style, not any style at all, but an enlightenment. Not
a conditioning of the mind, not a conditioning of the soul, but
an enlightenment of the mind concerning these things which
are fundamental to a culture of our own.

ARCHITECTURE AS CULTURE

1939

Architecture is that great living creative spirit which from generation to generation, from age to age, proceeds, persists, creates, according to the nature of man, and his circumstances as they both *change*. That really is architecture.

1954

There is no such thing as an architect who is but one thing, or limited in his views, in his outlook. He must be the most comprehensive of all the masters, the most comprehensive of all the human beings on earth. His work is the thing that is entrusted to him by way of his virtue, is most broad of all.

1931

If there is architecture in Mars or Venus, and there is, at least there is the architecture of Mars and Venus themselves—the same principles are at work there, too. Principles are universal.

Never miss the idea that architecture and music belong together.
They are practically one.

What I call integral ornament is founded upon the same organic
simplicities as Beethoven's *Fifth Symphony*, that amazing revolution
in tumult and splendor of sound built upon four tones, based
upon a rhythm a child could play on the piano with one finger.
Supreme imagination reared the four repeated tones, simple
rhythms, into a great symphonic poem that is probably the
noblest thought-built edifice in our world. And architecture
is like music in this capacity for the symphony.

What a great thing it would have been for us if, on the *Mayflower,*
there had been a genuine architect, a creative architect.

Architecture must now construct anew the whole social
pattern of our time as a new order of the human spirit.

Architecture is basic to culture. Music is an attribute of culture, so is painting, so would sculpture be. But architecture you experience; the other things you accede to. So without architecture you cannot have a culture.

I believe architecture to be the *humanizing* of building. The more humane, the more rich and significant, inviting and charming your architecture becomes, the more truly it is the great basis of a true culture.

PRACTICAL ADVICE

1953

The physician can bury his mistakes, but the architect can only advise his client to plant vines—so they should go as far as possible from home to build their first buildings.

1957

The cardinal sin in architecture is overdoing anything.

Rhythm in a building is largely a question of the third dimension or the depth of the building. A thing is out of place when it is not in rhythm. And what is rhythm in a building? In music you listen to it, in painting you look at it, in a building you live with it.

By way of innate sense of comfort, had come the idea that the size of the human figure should fix every proportion of a dwelling or of anything in it. Human scale was true building scale.

Sentimentality is, of course, sentiment gone to seed. Sentimentality is something dead and inexpressible. Stay away from it.

Decoration is intended to make use more charming and comfort more appropriate, or else a privilege has been abused.

A sense of proportion is a conscientious realization of limitation.

The traffic problem is the problem the architect must meet and solve first . . . Unless the motor car problem is first of all solved—approached and solved—I see no reason for building beautiful, expensive, monumental buildings.

ARCHITECT AS PRIEST

1949

The complete architect . . . is master of the elements: earth, air, fire, light, and water. Space, motion, and gravitation are his palette: the sun his brush. His concern is the heart of humanity. He, of all men, must see into the life of things; know their honor.

1955

When Jesus said "The Kingdom of God is within you" —within *you* there is the basis of organic thought, in architecture, too. The reality of the thing is the within, and it is within, and it radiates, and you feel it, and if you feel it strong enough, you can build it.

Architecture is a great spirit that has pervaded the world ever since man began to make marks on the wall of his cave and tried to make what he lived in consonant with his environment and beautiful. Savages seem to have made a better job of it than civilized people.

1937

IN ARCHITECTURE, AS IN LIFE, TO SEPARATE SPIRIT AND MATTER IS TO DESTROY BOTH.

REACTIONS

1957

Everybody goes to the Capitol in Washington and is impressed. Of course that is what the Capitol was built to do—to give humanity an inferiority complex.

1958

The prefabricated house is inevitable, and a good thing.

Poetic tranquility instead of a more deadly "efficiency,"
should be the consequence in the art of building: concordant,
sane, exuberant, and appropriate to purpose. Durable,
serviceable, economical. Beautiful.

I remember how as a boy, primitive American architecture
—Toltec, Aztec, Mayan, Inca—stirred my wonder, excited
my wishful admiration. I wished I might someday have money
enough to go to Mexico, Guatemala and Peru to join in
excavating those long slumbering remains of lost cultures;
mighty, primitive abstractions of man's culture—ancient
arts of the Mayan, the Inca, the Toltec . . . A grandeur arose
in the scale of total building never since excelled, seldom
equalled by man either in truth of plan or simple primitive
integrity of form. Architecture intrinsic to time, place and man.

1954

In nature there is a continuous, ceaseless becoming. There is the great in-between of which Lao-tze speaks, which is alive, which never ceases to be.

1931

Organic simplicity might be seen producing significant character in the harmonious order we call Nature—all around, beauty in growing things. None insignificant.

1954

Simplicity is a clean, direct expression of that thing which is itself. A wildflower has simplicity; a cultivated flower seldom has. Cultivation seems to go against that simplicity in the flower, and it does the same thing in human life.

1955

Nature is your book of reference, and in it you study and learn.

1955

Frederick Froebel, the founder of the kindergarten, declared you should not just go out and look at nature and draw these natural effects, but you should go into nature—find out the forms that are elemental.

1959

That which is according to nature survives. That which is contrary to nature disappears. As it is true to nature, there is where you place your platform, where you can put your feet, and stand there and never be deceived.

1957

Art is a discovery and development of elementary principles of nature into beautiful forms suitable for human use.

1953

YOU MIGHT SAY THAT NATURE IS THE GOD OF THE ARCHITECT.

1948

Go outdoors and look at the trees. See the specimens of foliage and new ones springing up all the while. Go in a garden and watch the flowers. It is just one principle—the principle is the same in every one, but see the enormous variety.

1956

The [Welsh] definition of genius was very simple, very true, and very good: A man who can see nature; a man who has a heart for nature (that is, who loves nature), and a man who had the courage to follow nature.

A flower is an intangible. It may be an eye looking out
on us from the great inner sea of beauty and precious
beyond words.

Conformity is the death of the thing nature would call life.

[If] you form the habit of nature study, little by little you will
find your faculties strengthened, refreshed, and capable of
more effective interpenetration, and it will go on as long as
you will.

My mother used to cut flowers with great long stems and put
them in glass [vases] always so she could see the stems in the
water, and I have inherited that—I like to see that, too.

When I say *nature* I do not mean the wind, and the bees and
the trees and the animals. I mean the nature with a capital
"N" is the essence of life everywhere, the essence of life itself.

Everything that is romantic is of nature.

THE SOUL
+ FAITH

1950

I do not believe you can build beautiful buildings, that true edifices can arise, except that they come from a worthy source, and that source is inevitably the human soul, the human heart.

1931

"BE CLEAN!" "BE CLEAN" WAS THE SOUL OF SHINTO. SHINTO SPOKE NOT OF A GOOD MAN, NOR SPOKE OF A MORAL MAN, BUT SPOKE OF A CLEAN MAN. SHINTO SPOKE NOT ONLY OF CLEAN HANDS, BUT OF A CLEAN HEART.

1952

I think that nothing can improve except as the soul improves, and if the soul improves the spirit radiates it immediately, because spirit radiates the soul.

1956

Integrity is the first law of the spirit.

Your soul is you and that soul produces what is called
your spirit . . . The soul is the essence of you, the essential
you. Your spirit is the temper, color, and expressiveness
of your soul.

Good reading of the great poets is just as essential to the
spiritual life as sitting down at the table and eating when
you are hungry.

THE MAIN THING IS TO KEEP AN OPEN MIND
AND A CONTRIBUTING SPIRIT, NOT GET
STIFFENED AND SHUTTING THINGS OUT,
BUT RECEPTIVE, WILLING, AND EAGER TO GET
HOLD OF WHAT IS TRUE AGAINST WHAT IS
FALSE. AND THAT IS THE BEST ROAD FORWARD.

1952

I am inclined to think that the time scale is a very serious impediment to the development of the interior quality of the human soul.

1951

This age we are living in is going to be known as the "Sanitary Age," the age in which we have bathtubs, water closets, and running water—and no soul.

1957

The recuperative power of the human frame, human body, if coupled with the right kind of spirit, is almost invincible.

1958

Your strength physically is nothing without the spiritual strength that should go with it.

1958

A man's conscience is really the mainspring of what he, with some reason, might call his soul. So listen attentively to conscience, always.

To have a cause and a loyalty at heart for a cause that is deep and profound will give your manhood a fine stance. You will be square on your spiritual feet.

There is a deadly tendency toward conformity which in the human spirit is something like gangrene in the human flesh.

I believe that incarnation is always and forever in some form or other. I do not think that we ever lose that incarnation. Now what forms it may take in afterlife, how that incarnation is to keep manifesting itself through the various changes of time in the universe, I do not know and I do not think anyone knows.

Really to believe in something is the greatest boon, I think, and to believe wholeheartedly in it and to serve it with all your strength and your might is salvation.

Respect the masterpiece—it is true reverence to man.
There is no quality so great, none so much needed now.

THE GREAT THING FOR US IS FAITH—
FAITH IN THE INCARNATION—FAITH IN
ITS QUALITY, IN ITS INEVITABILITY, IN ITS
INDESTRUCTIBILITY. THAT IS WHAT WE
CALL RELIGION—SHOULD CALL RELIGION.
AND THAT RELIGION IS THE GREATEST
RELIGION, WHICH GIVES YOU THE MOST
STRENGTH AND COURAGE IN THAT FAITH.

Lao-tze declared that as soon as anything became tangible,
it was dead. It is only the intangibles that are living and have
the power of becoming.

Einstein was the greatest of the scientists. He was the man who confessed that science would find—after all was done, all calculations on record, all achievements—that it was up to the final reality, and that reality was art and religion.

INSOFAR AS I AM IMMORTAL, I WILL BE IMMORTAL.

I don't see any reason why anyone should ever age; they can grow old in years; their faculties can diminish physically. But as they diminish physically, they should increase spiritually. And there is a compensation there that should make elderly people, people of experience, more and more valuable as they grow older, instead of less and less so.

I have an ideal and that ideal is all I ever expect to see of God, and I believe in my ideal so I believe in God.

I have talked of honest arrogance, but there is no such thing as honest arrogance. Arrogance is only arrogance when it has nothing under it, when it has nothing to stand on, when it is a pretense, a quackery, or a fake. When it is genuine it is a pride that is the highest form of humility we will ever know. It is evidence of a great faith in one's own ground, one's own star, a religious faith, perhaps, and that cannot be broken down and we should not call it arrogance.

HUMANITY

1954

Youth is a quality once you achieve you never lose it, and
I guess if you die with it, you are immortal.

1956

THE GREATEST HARM THAT MAN CAN DO IN LIFE IS TO SPOIL THE FAITH, THE TRUST, AND THE FRESH VISION OF THE CHILD.

1928

We hunger for POETRY naturally as we do for sunlight,
fresh air, and fruits, if we are normal human beings.

1951

What really does humanity want? Of course we know the
answer: three squares a day, fornication, and a good snore.
And above that, not much else.

1954

The great man is the man who deals in realities as the
intangibles of today.

1957

I think hardship is necessarily invaluable. Without it there could be no growth and I think that suffering is absolutely essential to growth.

1957

Arrogance is something a man possesses on the surface to defend the fact that he has not got the things he pretends to have. He's a bluff, in other words.

1957

If you are going to remain free, you must be free by way of your conscience and your ability to think.

1957

I DO NOT THINK WE SHOULD BE TOO CONTENT, TOO SATISFIED, WITH ANYTHING, AT ANYTIME, WHATSOEVER.

Sentiment is an honorable, desirous state. Now when you become sentimental, then that is the good thing gone over the board, gone wrong, and where an excess ruins its integrity and its beauty.

The one great truth of which mankind could be certain: that all was to change; that all was in a process of change; and the law of change was the valid, visible law which man could comprehend.

Humanity cannot exist without a love of and a sense of and a desire for the superior thing.

The uncommon man is the man who can fall in love with an idea, the man who can subscribe to an idea and who realizes the nature of an idea.

Ridicule is just that of the buffoon. Ridicule is something on the surface and much easier to practice and what you usually get in the name of humor.

Humor is pathos, never far from tears. You can laugh and cry when you laugh.

No man climbs so high or sinks so low that he is not eager to receive the good will and admiration of his fellow man. He may hitch his wagon to a star and, however he may be circumstanced or whatever his ideals or his actions, he never loses the desire for the approbation of his kind.

You can only become extrovert as you have been introvert, that is, as you have been perceptive, as you have perceived, taken into yourself, something you can give.

Humor has in it something close to tears; it goes deep into human nature.

I do think that a sense of humor is one of the most valuable things you can possess.

HUMAN NATURE IS SO CONSTRUCTED THAT IT HAS AN INNATE SYMPATHY WITH THOSE THINGS WITH WHICH IT HAS ASSOCIATED JOY, DIGNITY, AND GOOD LUCK.

As the squeeze comes on . . . the truth comes out; and so, with adversity as the hammer, the forge is in which the character is made.

When the struggle ends, and when there is no longer a demand upon your faculties to surmount, to achieve, and to become, you are dead.

WISDOM

1957

I lived with all the expressions of beauty I could see.
And all those that I could acquire and use for study and
enjoyment I acquired as my library, but living with them
all as I might.

1931

A matter of taste is usually a matter of ignorance.

1954

A man is wise from within . . . and from that within comes
this mystical quality of the human soul which we call wisdom.

1954

Honor your father and mother always, and don't believe
what you read in the newspapers.

—Letter to Janice Kimberlin, 6th grade

1955

Education, of course, is always based upon what was.
Education shows you what has been and leaves you to
make the deduction as to what may be. Education as
we pursue it can not prophesy, and does not.

1956

One should never dwell on one's failures. You should think about them only enough to gain the wisdom from them that they will afford.

1956

THE FRESH MIND SEES WITH A SEEING EYE AND IS LIKELY TO SEE TRUTH. BUT THE MORE YOU ARE EDUCATED AND THE MORE YOU ARE CONDITIONED, THE LESS ABLE YOU BECOME TO SEE STRAIGHT.

1955

True education in architecture, in anything else, would consist in the ability to respond to and appreciate the beautiful, and to consider it as the highest and the finest kind of morality.

1958

True study is a form of experience.

1957

Publicity seems to be the blood circulating in the intellectual veins of the nation.

I think the only basis for criticism is love, a feeling of love for the thing that you are talking about and you are expressing. Only as you *understand* that thing have you any right to criticize.

An expert is a man who has stopped thinking because "he knows."

Wisdom in the human-bud becomes fragrance in the human flower.

Emerson today is the strongest, purest, finest mind this country has ever produced, and everybody should read him daily.

Cultivate the poet. The poet is the unacknowledged legislator of this universe and the sooner we knock under to that the better. Get Emerson's essay on the American scholar and read it once a year.

1950

Love is only a kind of understanding. What you understand is the extent and the measure of your power to love anything.

1952

A great architect is not made by way of a brain nearly so much as by way of a cultivated, enriched heart. It is the love of the thing that he does that really qualifies him in the end.

1956

The inferior mind always tries to learn by comparison, but the deeper mind, the good mind, learns by analysis.

1957

If you are going to read, you should read something that will feed you, build you up, strengthen you and be what you need to know.

1956

The present system of education is the trampling of the herd.

1958

Never have I thought of an educated man as a cultured man, a cultured human being.

If you have actual knowledge concerning certain truths
in relation to building or painting or music or sculpture,
those are the things that will grow and endure and
eventually persist.

Culture is developed from within and education is to be
groomed from without.

The old academic order is bulging with its own
important impotence.

FEAR IS USUALLY COUPLED, AND INEVITABLY IS, WITH IGNORANCE.

A marital bureau and a trade school is what the universities,
so called, have degenerated to in our country.

When anyone becomes an authority, that is the end of him
so far as development is concerned.

AN IDEA IS SALVATION BY IMAGINATION.

There is nothing so inspiring to the spirit of a boy who wants to design something as a beautiful stretch, a blank sheet of paper, T square, triangle, and a pencil.

May your own genius inspire and keep you as a blessing to your time and place.

—Letter to former apprentice Andrew Devane

When you become the pencil in the hand of the infinite, when you are truly creative in your attempt to design, the thing that we call good design begins and never has an end. Once you are aware of the importance of this spirit living in nature, you will never have to copy nature.

I think the worst thing that can happen is to publish your work prematurely.

It is those *little* things that you do and that you do with your feeling and with your heart that are really constructive.

Invention is not creation. To invent something is not creative.

CREATION IS SOMETHING WITHIN, THE NATURE OF AN EXPERIENCE MOVING OUTWARD INTO LIFE WITH GREAT CONSEQUENCES.

This design matter is not something to do with a drawing board. It is something you do as you work, as you play. You may get it in the middle of the tennis court, and drop your racket, run off, and put it down. That is the kind of thing that it is. It is fleeting; it is evanescent.

To be creative as an individual you must be in yourselves qualified. And to be qualified, you must have quality.

It is imitation of imitation that destroys an original tradition. To be loyal to tradition, you have to understand it as a great central motivating factor.

Too much success, too much ease, too much food, too much of anything, is the end of the creative endeavor.

Vision has to have some guidance and motivation or it will simply see things as they are, not as they ought to be.

The song, the masterpiece, the edifice are a warm outpouring of the heart of man—human delight in life triumphant: we glimpse the infinite.

1958

There is no artist without his religion, without his philosophy, without his faith in mankind.

1959

I do not think you are a real photographer until you develop your own plates, because in the development comes a great deal of the effect.

1952

There is no such thing as an artist without a philosophy.

C. 1957

Creative instinct belongs to the human race. It has manifested itself in so many different ways down the ages—Oriental, Western, modern, southern, northern. It has all come from the same source, the same stream. And that source is not the brain, it is not the head, it is not the intellect—it is the heart. It is the warmth of heart and the love of life, that really is the best mainspring for an artist creating anything, no matter what it is.

I HAVE NEVER WANTED TO BE FINISHED.
I HAVE NEVER WANTED TO FEEL THAT WHAT
I HAVE DONE WAS THE BEST I COULD DO . . .
I HAVE TO BE CAREFUL OF THAT BECAUSE
THAT IS POISON TO THE CREATIVE SPIRIT.

The moment a thing becomes a fixed point, it is dead.
The true living thing is always in between and in a state
of becoming.

BEAUTY

1952

As beautiful building after beautiful building gets itself constructed and built, they will begin to look into it and try to find out what the secret was that kept it perennially young and always working and never let it die because it couldn't die. A principle never dies.

1954

I BELIEVE A HOUSE IS MORE A HOME BY BEING A WORK OF ART.

1952

Could you imagine anything more dreary than modern civilization without anything of beauty in it at all? Just what they call practical. I cannot think of anything more dead, more stupid, more of a thing I'd like to get away from.

1951

The thing that is lost to us most completely now, I think, is the capacity to draw the line between what is merely curious and what is really beautiful.

What is good in our present civilization is still a hankering after something beautiful.

Color has a significance all its own, and in a realm all its own. Just as music has, color is the music of light.

A civilization can occur by way of science, and science can maintain a civilization up to a certain point. But culture is a way of making that way of life which is a civilization beautiful.

I believe that Emerson was right when he said, "Beauty is the highest and finest kind of morality." If you are attuned— and you love sincerely—harmony, rhythm, and what we call beauty, instinctively what is ugly will become offensive to you. It will come into the realm of the spirit also. You will see how certain actions of your own are ugly, how certain of others are beautiful.

1955

A man without a sense of beauty is like a ship without a rudder: no place to go but out and no place to come but back.

1956

Instinctively and naturally, if you beautify your own life, you beautify the life of everybody around you.

1949

It is the *quality* in things that should make them desirable and beautiful, the joy forever that is ever and will always be the most important thing to mankind.

1928

COLORS—IN PASTE OR CRAYON—OR PENCILS—ALWAYS A THRILL! TO THIS DAY I LOVE TO HOLD A HANDFUL OF MANY-COLORED PENCILS AND OPEN MY HAND TO SEE THEM LYING LOOSE UPON MY PALM, IN THE LIGHT.

1957

We are all here to develop a life more beautiful, more concordant, more fully expressive of our own sense of pride and joy than ever before in the world.

1957

To make anything beautiful is to make it naturally lovable, for it to have charm, for it to be genuine, for it to be an expression of all that is worth having or worth living for in our universe today.

1952

THE ELEMENT OF COLOR—IT IS ANOTHER WORLD. THAT PROBABLY IS THE MOST MYSTERIOUS WORLD OF ALL—EVEN MORE MYSTERIOUS THAN FORM.

1957

When you have the sense of the whole, as harmonious, then you begin to express what we call the beautiful and you yourselves become artists.

Nothing is worth a man's time—and that means a woman's —except a search for the beautiful, and an attempt to establish it in human life by way of the human being and his existence.

If you want a friend and counselor and guide, there is one, and that lies in the heart, not so much in the head. It is the love of beauty, the desire in your heart to leave this place into which you were born a better place to live in because you lived there, and because you have lived as you have lived.

When you are on the track of an origin, which is a wonderful track to pursue, you will get back to the fact that the earlier the thing occurred, in the first simplicity of the burst forth of the idea, that was when it was most effective, most beautiful.

CULTURE
+VALUES

1951

A CULTURE IS THE JOY OF LIVING, AND THE BEAUTY OF LIVING.

1950

I never like to think back to Rome, because Rome was already degenerate, and I think Rome in its day was where we are in our day.

1953

A civilization is just a way of life, and there have been hundreds of them, thousands of them in the world. But a culture is the way of making that life beautiful.

1951

Culture has always been an import. Very seldom has culture ever sprung from the ground by way of a native.

1956

Culture means taking the thing according to its nature, giving it freedom, and the thing that it loves most and best and encouraging it to grow, and giving it materials to grow with.

The artist himself, of course, is of his time, or he is not an artist. He is the prophet of his time and of his day; he is the seeing-eye of his people. He can see a little further and more clearly than his people see. That is why he is an artist. That is why the prophetic poet is the greater of all the members of his civilization.

CONSCIENCE IS REALLY THE SOUL OF FREEDOM.

I firmly believe that if you give the right thing to people to see and really experience, they will choose the right thing.

The world has never had a culture until it had an architecture. The architecture was the basis of its culture, rather than the culture the basis of its architecture.

1954

In any final result there can be no separation between our architecture and our culture. Nor any separation of either from our happiness. Nor any separation from our work.

1957

I respect any man or woman who respects himself sufficiently to tell the truth no matter what or who it might hurt.

1959

The growth of your souls, the expression of that thing that is you, is a matter of culture.

1952

Quality consists in a developed consciousness and in a capacity for complete correlation of your faculties. If you are not a correlated human being, you are fragmentary, you are awkward, you are not there in any sense with the thing that is needed to be there.

1958

Your conscience is your guiding star and the finest thing about you in principle where manhood or womanhood is concerned.

1952

Principles are always major. Ways and means are always minor, and they will arrange themselves in relation to the center line of principle.

1956

Conscience and freedom are inalienable companions.

1952

Morals are the customs which are conceded to be, or considered to be, at that time, the good ones as against the bad ones. When we say a moral man we mean a man who, according to the tenor and judgment of his time, does the right thing. But it may not be, in any ethical analysis, the true thing.

1931

The working of a principle is the only safe tradition.

1952

When you speak of ethics, then you are getting to the actual organic nature of right and wrong. Ethics and morality have very little in common.

1953

It is so easy when you know a principle to allow that principle to work for you and to do astonishingly sound and beautiful new expressions. Because there is no end to that.

1956

QUALITY AND QUANTITY ARE NOT ON SPEAKING TERMS—NEVER CAN BE.

1957

There is no substitute for intrinsic responsibility, innate responsibility for your own acts, for your own character, and for your own self.

1957

The best denial is the right affirmation.

DEMOCRACY
+ THE
INDIVIDUAL

DEMOCRACY CAN LIVE BY GENIUS ONLY. ITS VERY SOUL IS INDIVIDUALITY.

There is no such thing as creative except by the individual. Humanity, especially on a democratic basis, lives only by virtue of individuality.

I believe the man is more a man by being an individual rather than a committee-meeting.

I do not believe in force, and I do not believe in ganging up on anything. I believe in individuality and the power and effect of the individual's convictions and contributions.

Everyone professing democracy should have not only an open mind but a certain charity of the soul that appreciates the qualities in others.

We are beginning to learn that the highest and finest kind of morality is beauty, and that there is no culture for democracy until it has one of its own.

NATURE IS MANIFESTLY IN LOVE WITH WHAT WE CALL INDIVIDUALITY. INDIVIDUALITY IS SOMETHING PRECIOUS IN THIS WORLD TO BE PRESERVED, AND I WOULD HATE TO SEE ANY OF IT SACRIFICED IN SOME FOOLISH ENDEAVOR IN THE DIRECTION OF "INTERNATIONALISM."

1957

Paradise for me would be a democracy where the poetic principle was inviolate and . . . the basis of all judgments. The new integrity.

GOVERNMENT

1954

I think that government is totally unqualified to take a hand in culture. Culture, so far as government is concerned, never was a matter that would be legitimate in its hands.

1955

FEAR IS THE ELEMENT THROUGH WHICH WE ARE GOVERNED, AND THAT IS WHY WE HAVE GOVERNMENT TODAY—BECAUSE FEAR IS EFFECTIVE.

1957

I think one war only breeds another, and I have been borne out by a reading of history. One war always has in its intestines another, and another has another.

1956

To place too great an emphasis on the common man is to glorify mediocrity.

1957

HUMANITY, TO ME, IS NOT A MOB. THE MOB IS THE DEGENERATION OF HUMANITY, THE MOB IS HUMANITY GOING THE WRONG WAY.

1957

If we were all aware of the principle of humanity by which we live, war would have no being—there would be no war. If statesmanship truly represented the sentiment of the people themselves, there would be no war.

It is notorious that the human animal is of such a character and nature that he cannot be trusted with authority. And just when we need quality the most, here comes mediocrity rising into high places. We have the domination of the mediocre.

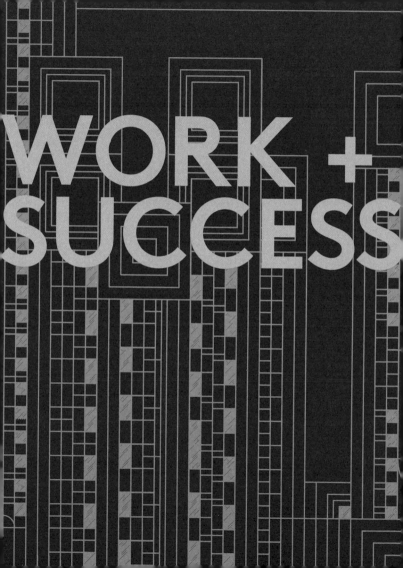

1954

What a man does—*that* he has. You may find other things on him but they are not his.

1957

There is no real development without integrity, that is— a love of truth.

1957

I consider myself a success only insofar as my life is useful, revealing, and rewarding to my kind.

1950

I BELIEVE THAT IN THE SEARCH FOR THE ANSWER LIES THE ANSWER.

1952

Principles are limitations because in the principle lies direction. Principles are hard masters, and you need to know that in order to do great work, work that will stand.

If you have not had experience in connection with the thing that you are doing, you are going to make a fool of yourself or somebody else. Probably all together.

I am sure if I had not elected to live with my work, I never could have done even half what I have accomplished. I think that is the secret of really being productive, is to stay with it.

I DO NOT BELIEVE YOU KNOW WHAT FUN IS UNTIL YOU KNOW WHAT HARD WORK IS. I THINK THAT OUT OF THAT REFLEX FROM HARD WORK COMES REAL FUN, COMES REAL ENJOYMENT OF THE THINGS THAT ARE MORE EXCELLENT, THE THINGS THAT ARE POETRY AND THE THINGS THAT ARE MUSIC AND THE THINGS THAT ARE BEAUTY.

You have to go wholeheartedly into anything in order to achieve anything worth having.

You do not learn by way of your successes. No one does. Your successes gradually build a wall between you and your creative self. You cannot afford to let that happen. You must always keep that wall aside so that you can see out.

According to our strength of character and our clarity of vision, we will endure, we will succeed, we will have contributed something to make life where we were and as we lived it, something a little better, brighter, and more beautiful.

WRIGHT
ON
WRIGHT

I NEVER HAD THE COURAGE TO LIE.

1951

My father was a preacher and musician. He taught me to regard a symphony as an edifice of sound. And ever since I have been listening to the great orchestras of the world as I would look at a building.

1955

If you were to deduct Froebel,* Goethe, Beethoven, and Nietzsche from my education, I should be very much the poorer.

1951

I wanted to be developed into an individual capable of honoring the profession I was in, not selling it down the river.

---

* Friedrich Froebel (1782–1852) was a German educational innovator whose ideas influenced Frank Lloyd Wright's mother, Anna Lloyd Jones Wright.

I know in my own case that nothing has been of any great value or lasting benefit to me or anybody else except as I have put my feet down where I could do something to make the world a little more beautiful.

I HAD TO CHOOSE EARLY IN MY LIFE BETWEEN AN HONEST ARROGANCE AND A HYPOCRITICAL HUMILITY, AND I DELIBERATELY CHOSE AN HONEST ARROGANCE.

I never sit down to a drawing board—and this has been a lifelong practice of mine—until I have the whole thing in my mind. I may alter it substantially, I may throw it away, I may find I'm up a blind alley, but unless I have the idea pretty well in shape, you won't see me at the drawing board with it.

To cut ambiguity short: there never was exterior influence upon my work, either foreign or native, other than that of Lieber Meister,★ Dankmar Adler and John Roebling, Whitman and Emerson, and the great poets worldwide. My work is original not only in fact but in spiritual fiber. No practice by any European architect to this day has influenced mine in the least.

I believe myself that I have learned from my mistakes the most. You will never learn anything from your successes, but from your mistakes you will get an education.

I have never in my life gone to anybody for a job. I have never turned my hand that much to ask a friend to say a word for me for a job, and yet I survive.

★ The man whom Wright called Leiber Meister ("beloved master") was Louis Sullivan (1856–1924), a celebrated architect for whom Wright worked as a draftsman.

Japanese prints as I first saw them changed my way of looking at nature.

I have never had any greater pleasure than to take a handful of colored pencils in one hand here, T square and triangle lying on a sheet of white paper, and try to feel the design of the thing I want to do. It's a great moment.

Romance is the flowering of the spirit, the flowering of the soul of man. It is of the man, of the circumstance, of the nature and the character of whatever he is himself . . . I have always confessed and represented myself as a romantic architect because romance is organic.

I have been black and blue in some spot, somewhere, almost all my life from too intimate contact with my own early furniture.

I AM NOT A "MASTERPIECE MAN"—
THE NEXT ONE I AM GOING TO DO IS
ALWAYS THE BEST. WHEN A MAN POINTS
TO HIS MASTERPIECE, HE IS FINISHED.
DO NOT LOOK FOR MUCH FROM HIM.

1952

I have been practicing architecture some sixty-one years, and I can still feel that all I need is another chance to do a good building. The next one will be it.

QUOTATION
SOURCES

(ALL WORKS BY FRANK LLOYD WRIGHT UNLESS OTHERWISE NOTED.)

AML = Brownell, Baker, and Frank Lloyd Wright. *Architecture and Modern Life*. New York: Harper, 1937.

AU = *An Autobiography*. Petaluma, CA: Pomegranate, 2005.

CD = *Frank Lloyd Wright: The Crowning Decade, 1949–1959*. Selected and with commentary by Bruce Brooks Pfeiffer. Fresno: Press at California State University, Fresno, 1989.

CW1 = *Collected Writings, Volume 1, 1894–1931*. Edited by Bruce Brooks Pfeiffer. New York: Rizzoli, 1992.

CW2 = *Collected Writings, Volume 2, 1930–1932*. Edited by Bruce Brooks Pfeiffer. New York: Rizzoli, 1992.

CW3 = *Collected Writings, Volume 3, 1931–1939*. Edited by Bruce Brooks Pfeiffer. New York: Rizzoli, 1993.

HLV = *Frank Lloyd Wright: His Living Voice*. Selected and with commentary by Bruce Brooks Pfeiffer. Fresno: Press at California State University, Fresno, 1987.

MA = *Modern Architecture, Being the Kahn Lectures for 1930.* Princeton Monographs in Art and Archaeology. Princeton, NJ: Princeton University Press, 1931.

NH = *The Natural House.* New York: Horizon, 1954.

TE = *A Testament.* New York: Horizon, 1957.

TL = *Two Lectures on Architecture.* Chicago: Art Institute of Chicago, 1931.

TT = Transcript of tape recordings made of Frank Lloyd Wright speaking between 1949 and 1959. Frank Lloyd Wright Foundation Archives, Taliesin West, Scottsdale, Arizona.

WD = *When Democracy Builds.* Chicago: University of Chicago, 1945.

(ABBREVIATIONS REFER TO PRECEDING LIST OF SOURCES.)

ARCHITECTURE: CW1, 340; TT no. 95, 5–6; TT no. 235, 21; MA, endpaper; CW1, 340; TT no. 251, 5; TT no. 270, 22; TT no. 96, 36; TL, 49; CW3, 331; TT no. 280, 2; CW2, 51; NH, 16; CW3, 223; Frank Lloyd Wright, *Marin County Civic Center* (San Francisco: Royal Blueprint Company, 1957), no page numbers; TT no. 259, 3; CW1, 127; NH, 218–219; "Frank Lloyd Wright Talks on His Art," *New York Times Magazine,* October 4, 1953, 47; WD, 53; TT no. 258, 9; CW3, 331; TT no. 110, 16–17; TL, 49; TT no. 277, 28; Elizabeth Gordon, "The Symphonic Poem of a Great House," *House Beautiful,* November 1955, 272; TT no. 213, 8; Frank Lloyd Wright, "Recollections—United States, 1893–1920," *Architects Journal of London,* August 6, 1936, 174; TT no. 51, 11; TT no. 267, 12–13; "Frank Lloyd Wright Talks on His Art," *New York Times Magazine*, October 4, 1953, 47; TT no. 187, 1; TT no. 44, 28; NH, 17; TT no. 242, 12; AU, 145; HLV, 205; TT no. 291, 4; CW4, 382; TT no. 144, 23; TT no. 142, 9; AML, 45; HLV, 206; TT no. 195, 8; TT no. 205, 3; TE, 223; TE, 111–112.

NATURE: HLV, 178; TL, 13; TT no. 96, 39; TT no. 125, 25; TT no. 129, 10; TT no. 230, 19; TT no. 192, 6; TT no. 60, 3; TT no. 282, 18; TT no. 173, 4; TT no. 105, 2; TT no. 180, 20; TT no. 192, 22; TT no. 203, 13; TT no. 231, 17; TT no. 192, 9.

THE SOUL + FAITH: TT no. 256, 5; MA, 33; TT no. 47, 21; TT no. 158, 17; TT no. 47, 20; TT no. 146, 9; TT no. 232, 7; TT no. 55, 7; TT no. 26, 27; TT no. 204, 5; ibid.; TT no. 225, 5; TT no. 225, 10; TT no. 242, 13; TT no. 47, 22; HLV, 203; TL, 63; TT no. 47, 23; TT no. 199, 16; TT no. 233, 4; TT no. 299 (Mike Wallace interview), 310; TT no. 10, 4; TT no. 58, 9; TT no. 286, 8.

HUMANITY: TT no. 104b, 2; TT no. 152, 9; CW1, 314; TT no. 20, 10; TT no. 105, 2; TT no. 180, 5; CD, 80; TT no. 200, 9; TT no. 186, 11; TT no. 110, 16; TT no. 114, 10; TT no. 144, 13; TT no. 217, 5; TT no. 91, 3; TT no. 215, 5; TT no. 264, 1; TT no. 281, 25; TT no. 91, 3; TT no. 215, 6; TT no. 282, 21; TT no. 114, 8; TT no. 114, 9.

WISDOM: TE, 207; MA, endpaper; TT no. 110, 8–9; Frank Lloyd Wright to Janice Kimberlin (a sixth grader), March 6, 1954, Frank Lloyd Wright Foundation Archives, Taliesin West, Scottsdale, Arizona; TT no. 125, 8; TT no. 173, 10–11; TT no. 152, 9; TT no. 134, 9; TT no. 213, 11; TT no. 199, 6; TT no. 133, 3; Frank Lloyd Wright to Ralph Nader, December 24, 1957, Frank Lloyd Wright Foundation Archives, Taliesin West, Scottsdale, Arizona; CD, 90; TT no. 23, 2; TT no. 276a, 227; TT no. 4, 3; TT no. 46, 5; TT no. 160, 19; TT no. 299 (Mike Wallace interview), 309. TT no. 162, 10; TT no. 217, 5; TT no. 230, 19; TT no. 231, 9; NH, 32; TT no. 56, p. 12; TT no. 281, 20; TT no. 285, 6.

CREATIVITY: TL, 11; TT no. 204, 10; Frank Lloyd Wright to former apprentice Andrew Devane, March 27, 1956, Frank Lloyd Wright Foundation Archives, Taliesin West, Scottsdale, Arizona; HLV, 178; TT no. 12, 3; TT no. 133, 11; TT no. 41, 15; TT no. 29, 2; TT no. 113, 11; TT no. 50, 14; TT no. 62, 6; TT no. 114, 9; TT no. 139, 7; TL, 59; TT no. 207, 13; TT no. 233, 10; TT no. 58, 25; TT no. 260, 5; TT no. 46, 7; TT no. 183, 14.

BEAUTY: TT no. 44, 5; NH, endpaper; HLV, 123; TT no. 15, 13; TT no. 125, 19; TT no. 261, 11; TT no. 46, 22; TT no. 121, 8–9; TT no. 139, 15; TT no. 158, 15; CW4, 334; CW1, 269; T no. 183, 18; TT no. 198, 6; TT no. 45, 14; TT no. 203, 13; TT no. 241, 14; TT no. 258, 18; TT no. 228, 5.

CULTURE + VALUES: TT no. 26, 20; TT no. 12, 6–7; HLV, 105; TT no. 15, 4; TT no. 160, 4; TT no. 125, 7; TT no. 86, 9; TT no. 142, 14; TT no. 213, 7; NH, 51; CD, 81; TT no. 231, 9; TT no. 50, 15; TT no. 225, 5; TT no. 44, 34; TT no. 304, 10; TT no. 46, 8; MA, endpaper; TT no. 46, 9; TT no. 78, 10; TT no. 176, 11; TT no. 184, 12; TT no. 199, 14.

DEMOCRACY + THE INDIVIDUAL: CW1, 159; TT no. 113, 7; NH, endpaper; TT no. 176, 20; TT no. 50, 2; TT no. 297, 1; TT no. 282, 16; Frank Lloyd Wright to Lynn Farnol, July 12, 1957, Frank Lloyd Wright Foundation Archives, Taliesin West, Scottsdale, Arizona.

GOVERNMENT: TT no. 117, 15; TT no. 139, 17; TT no. 299 (Mike Wallace interview), 294; TT no. 155, 3; TT no. 299 (Mike Wallace interview), 307; TT no. 181, 32; TT no. 201, 11.

WORK + SUCCESS: NH, 24; TT no. 180, 20; CD, 48; TT no. 12, 9; TT no. 44, 32; TT no. 71, 7; TT no. 204, 7; TT no. 213, 12; TT no. 225, 2; TT no. 46, 7; TT no. 110, 11.

WRIGHT ON WRIGHT: TE, 207; TT no. 23, 3; TT no. 129, 12; TT no. 18, 25; TT no. 275, 13; TT no. 241, 12; TT no. 113, 10; TE, 205; TT no. 26, 14; TT no. 257, 14; TT no. 41, 17; TT no. 81, 15–16; TT no. 191, 6–7; NH, 43; TT no. 260, 11; TT no. 57, 28.